Experiments in Art

Donald L. Stacy

Experiments in Art

Four Winds Press • New York

Published by Four Winds Press
A Division of Scholastic Magazines, Inc., New York, N.Y.
Copyright © 1975 by Donald L. Stacy

Library of Congress Cataloging in Publication Data

Stacy, Don.
  Experiments in art.

  SUMMARY: An introduction to the techniques of
collage, printmaking, and drawing with suggestions
for projects.
    1. Art—Technique—Juvenile literature.
[1. Art—Technique] I. Title.
N7430.S82   702'.8   75-9551
ISBN 0-590-07332-X

CONTENTS

INTRODUCTION

Art is an experiment in surprising one's self. Each new combination of tools and materials that you try can create a different picture idea. That is why each set of projects in this book is based upon the use of certain materials. Try them all, for no one knows in advance which one will produce the best picture.

Remember that the examples and suggestions given are very general. You must experiment with each one, trying variations and combinations of your own that are unexpected. With practice, your ability to "picture" will grow along with control of the tools and materials.

Cutting, tearing, and pasting paper is a way of making designs without having to draw. You can make a whole form directly from a sheet of colored paper without drawing. Another advantage to paper tearing is that it is easier to change the composition of a picture—you can simply move things about. Six buildings, for example, can be picked up and shifted from the right side of the picture to the left, or one that was behind the others can be moved to the front. In this way the placement of objects is kept loose until you find the arrangement you like best.

Color, black-and-white tones, as well as textures can also be used in new ways. Certain bits of colored paper will seem to glow when next to one another. You must find these things out by doing them. Once you have discovered them, you can use all these effects to create your own pictures.

Print techniques offer another alternative to drawing. Once you realize that any raised or rough surface can be printed, the house becomes loaded with marvelous picture possibilities. If a piece of paper is placed on a coin and the surface is rubbed with a pencil or crayon, the image is transferred to the paper. In the same way, a textured wood grain found on the floor, a rough brick surface, even cloth or plastic fabrics have raised surface qualities that could be inked and printed. And many simple things can be placed directly into ink or paint and "stamped" in the same way that you would use a rubber stamp. This is a way of working with graspable materials. Things are actually arranged or made in order to print.

Once you are able to make complex and surprising things happen, you will try to use a little more control. Drawing helps place things *somewhere*. A simple line not only describes the edge of something, like a tree, but it puts the tree far back into the picture or brings it up very close. A line controls all kinds of change in size and feeling. It shows things can go under and over each other. Most important, a line is the best way to "write" down your picture ideas. It is the artist's shorthand.

Besides the experiments that take place on flat paper, some projects that include whole objects and three-dimensional form are important. A *feeling* of depth becomes actual depth. All kinds of real, tangible things can be used. The surprise happens when ordinary spools and boxes become something else.

In touching these three-dimensional or sculptural forms, a new tool is added. Our fingers "see" along with our eyes!

None of these art forms are new. They come from man's long history of art. Some painting and carving found in caves are over 20,000 years old! But even here there are marvelous images of animals. Paintings done on walls are called murals and are found in great temples, churches, and palaces in all parts of the world. The Greek temples, which are all bleached white, originally were painted with bright colors. Even the statues were painted. When books were made by hand, the lettering and illustrations were works of art. Later, printing became another kind of art form.

Art is found wherever man is or has been. It is a natural part of man. It is a kind of speech, a visual "talking." Enjoy this new type of expression and increase your ability to "say" things.

COLLAGE

Materials needed.
Paper paste and a brush with which to apply it; scissors; paper of all kinds, including wall paper samples, pages torn from magazines with bright colored designs, newspaper photos and lettering, tissues and metallic foils; fabrics; a paper punch; colored markers; inks or any water-based colors, including acrylic paints.

Collage is pasting flat materials such as paper and fabric onto a surface in order to make a picture or design. Since this idea became popular in Paris in the early twentieth century, when Picasso and Braque combined pasted paper and paint in their abstract work, the French word *colle,* meaning glue, was used for this technique.

Since then many artists have used collage, including Jean Dubuffet, Max Ernst, Paul Klee, and Kurt Schwitters.

A still life is a group of nonmoving objects. So think of a number of ordinary things that are not too difficult to make. In order to create something startling of such plain objects they need to be presented in a dramatic way. This means that extremes in color and texture must be used. They must also be large forms, as if seen very close up, otherwise there will be a lot of empty space that will lessen the impact of the simple forms. Choose your papers or materials with care so that bold patterns can be made to stand out against a finer detailed pattern. If you tear some of the edges and cut others with scissors, the contrast of edges will also increase the drama of the composition.

For a more complex design, interlock the cutout shapes. Instead of just pasting them one over the other, from the back to the front, snip them so that they are interwoven, like clasped hands.

For something more experimental make your own textured papers. Use many sheets of paper and scribble, drip, blot, or stain each one. Use markers and water colors. Then tear or cut them into forms that make up an amusing or pleasing image. When mounted on a sheet of one color they will stand out with greater clarity.

Sometimes it is fun to use actual pictures cut from magazines. A street scene or landscape will take on a surprising change of scale and mood if an image of yourself, or a friend, is included. Use an old unwanted photo and put yourself in the picture.

One of the good things about collage is the ease with which the shapes can be moved about before being pasted down. Shift the pieces around until they look best. Keep them from being too balanced or evenly spaced. Place large against small, horizontal against vertical. Then hold them in place with tacks or small weighted objects. Run a little paste on the tip of a brush under the loose edges to glue them to the background sheet.

A simple group of cutout rectangles can be easily turned into buildings. When a number of different kinds and sizes of letters are added, they become signs. All together they form a busy street full of shops and advertising.

You will notice that some colored papers blend together in a soft harmonious manner. More contrasting colors will clash and jump away from each other. Use color and texture pattern to capture the *sounds* of a city.

G

PUZZLE

Zip Code

the world's

To attempt a systems approach in a few errors. We have moved into a stage of h it is utterly

problems are those of man and mankind. We sh

Creative Systems

It
enco
minis
Mini
walk
meet
be a
Dani
garss
last
Thul
Jourr
Rasn
Mitee
Thul
conti
He
but s
polar
repre

Much of the space in magazines and newspapers is taken up by words. If you look with care you will find many sizes and styles of letters. With a little imagination these become wonderful pictures. First make a collection of as many sorts as possible, then see what they suggest to you.

15

In this project, a group of letters is used to make a picture. By cutting out a specific shape, a horse for example, from a page of small, close-set letters, and pasting it on a plain back-ground, a strong image will result. If a typewriter is available, type one letter over and over until it fills the whole sheet. Or type a name or word, like the fat man made from the word fat. Lines can be added for detail.

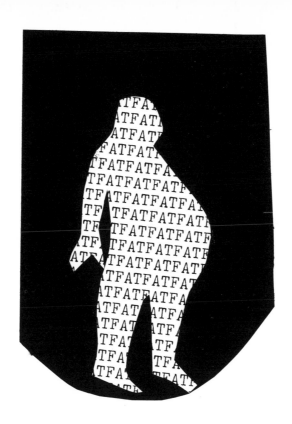

18

For a lovely Swiss-cheese effect, try this. Cut out some simple colored paper shapes. Next "punch" them all over with a paper punch. When these are combined with unpunched paper they will make a strong contrasting design. The background showing through the holes increases the feeling of color and of surprise.

By using a piece of black paper or board for a background, you can create the effect of stained glass. Any solid color will have this effect. Cut and place each colored shape so that there is a strip of background color showing around the outside of each one. Don't draw the design first. Let it develop as you go. Each shape can be changed, made a little larger or smaller, until it fits. Place the shapes so that the leftover "outline" is not quite even. Remember that the more variety in a picture the more interesting it is to the eye. The more contrasts and unexpected things, the better the surprise.

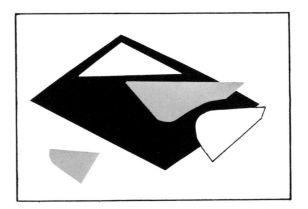

PRiNT TeCHNiQUES

Materials needed.
Cardboard; paper of all kinds; scissors; glue (an acrylic or waterproof type is best); sponges; string; ordinary or printing ink; water-based paint; brushes; rags; toothbrush; small flat objects.

Printing is a very early art form. When men wrote on clay tablets, carved seals were pressed into the damp clay as a kind of official signature. Later signet rings were designed to be pressed into hot wax in order to seal letters. A print is still called an impression. Many of the first printmakers in Europe, such as Albrecht Dürer, were trained in carving or incising jewelry. These printers cut very fine designs into blocks of hard wood. Ink was then rubbed over the surface and when the surface was pressed to paper, an image of the cut design was left. One block could make hundreds of prints. The invention of printed books took place when letters as well as pictures were hand carved.

If you look at a simple rubber stamp you will find the raised

---

letters are backward. All prints from a raised or relief surface make a reversed image. This really increases the sense of being surprised.

Many great artists used print making as a special type of expression. It has its own quality that makes it different from all other kinds of art work. Paintings take a long time to finish and can only be seen in one place, or owned by one person. Prints, however, are smaller and easier to move about. Since many prints can be made from one block, many people can have an identical hand printed original work of art. Even artists can collect each other's work. Modern artists are still experimenting with new ways of making prints.

You can make your own printing block from cardboard. A block is a base that holds the printing surface. Remember that only the high, or raised, parts will print, and the image will turn about or reverse.

23

Draw a design and cut it out of cardboard with scissors or a mat knife. Use a simple image for the best results. Glue the cut image to a base that is also of cardboard. This should be just a little larger than the cut design. Scratch the raised print surface to give it a texture. Brush a coat of glue over the whole thing and allow it to dry to make the printing block tougher and longer lasting.

For another kind of effect, there is available a special block printing ink that is applied with a rubber roller. However, plain writing or drawing ink or even water-based paint can be brushed over the surface. Place the paper carefully upon the wet block. Any slightly absorbent paper will do, although there are many fine rice papers that are made just for printing. Then rub the back of the paper with the flat of the hand or with a flat, firm object such as the handle of a wooden salad spoon.

Don't worry if the results are rough. Perfect printing is just as difficult as making the blocks. It takes a great deal of practice. Several must be done just to get the ink to soak into the board properly. These are called trial proofs.

Another kind of interesting print can be made by using ordinary flexible string. First apply a coat of glue to a rectangle of cardboard. Then, while it is still sticky, place string on it so as to form a design or image. Use a brush dipped in glue to force the string into place. Then ink and print the string design in the same way as the cardboard design.

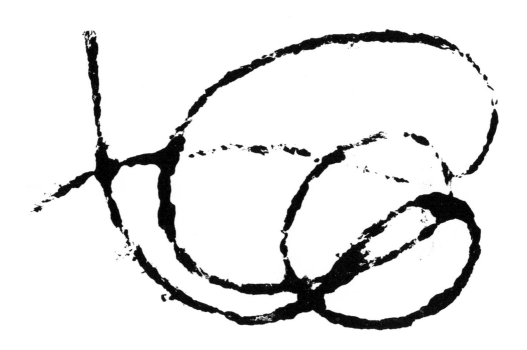

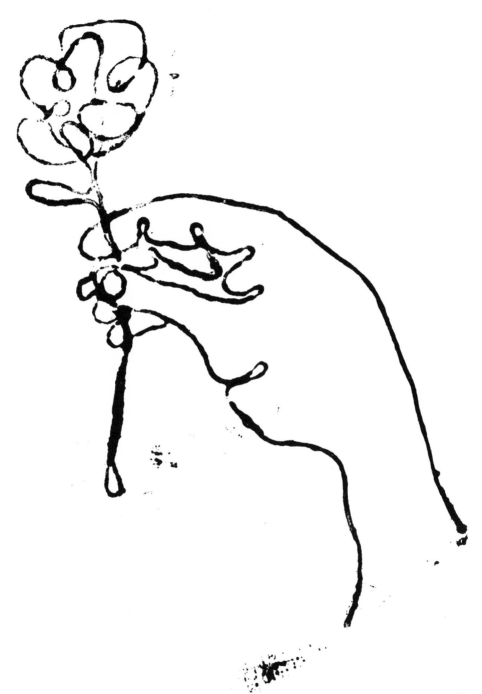

27

Glue itself can be used to make a texture and line print. Take some white glue that comes in a squeeze bottle or tube and lay out a line as though from a tube of toothpaste. When this is dry, brush more glue over the surface to leave slightly raised ridges and textures. When the block is dry cover it all with ink. Rub the back of the paper with something hard and flat, like the wooden spoon. Then rub the whole block softly using your hand or a rag. The hard raised lines will be almost white, or paper colored, since the glue resists water. The lower areas will hold enough ink to print all the brush marks. The exciting textures that result make the image seem to float in a sea of ink waves.

Stencils are another method of making prints. They can be made from slick-coated board like oak tag, or from ordinary board that has been given a coat of glue. Cut out the design and place it on top of the paper on which the print is to be made. Pour some ink into an old dish and dip a flat sponge into it. Pat the whole surface within the stencil gently with the inked sponge. The stencil will protect everything but the cut out area. When the stencil is removed, the design will appear. The same image can be stenciled over and over itself. One tree stencil can be used for a whole forest of trees. Again, remember that it may take a few tries to get the feel of this printing method.

Here is a variation of the stencil technique. Cut a stencil and place it on the paper you wish to print. Then take an old toothbrush, or small scrub brush, and dip it into the ink, or into paint that is thinned to the consistency of ink. Hold it in front of the areas to be filled and pull a flat stick or butter knife across the brush, toward you. This will create a mist of fine drops that fall over the design. When the opening is filled, lift the stencil up with care.

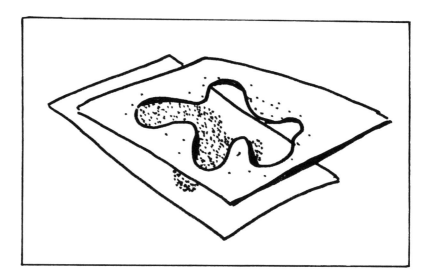

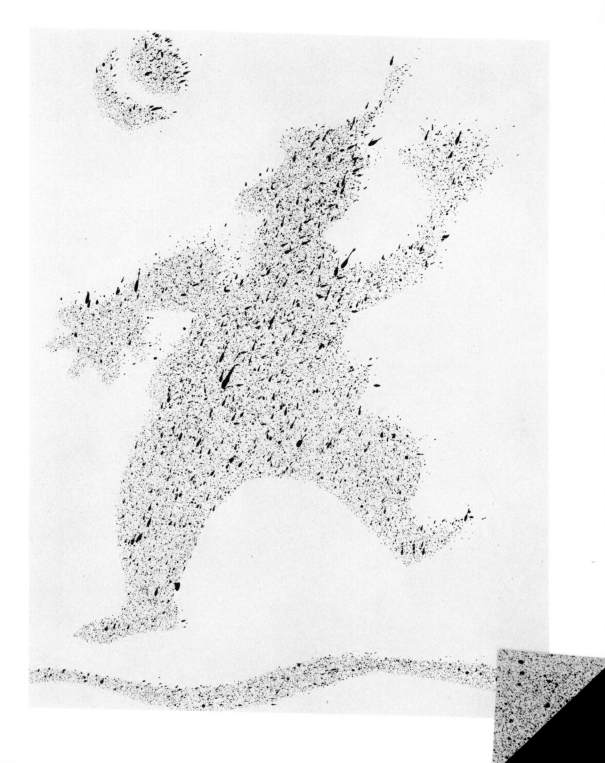

Instead of a cut stencil, try placing objects directly on the paper. You can use string, a hinge, sticks, keys, anything that has a good shape. Spray right over the whole "still-life." When the ink or paint is dry, lift each thing gently from the paper and see what kind of impression, or negative image they have left.

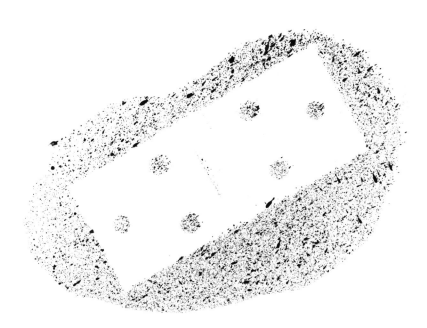

Objects themselves can also be printed directly. Any small thing can be dipped into paint, or patted with a sponge that has been inked, and then pressed to paper. Experiment with cut up sponges, children's blocks, clock or tool parts, leaves, and so on. The impression that is left is like that of a rubber stamp, but each material will take the ink differently. Since only one print can be done that is exactly like another, these are called monoprints.

For a real surprise take a wrinkled piece of cloth, dip it into black paint, and squash it down onto the paper. Try four or five times until an unusual image appears. Add some lines if you like. Different fabrics will give different results, so try several.

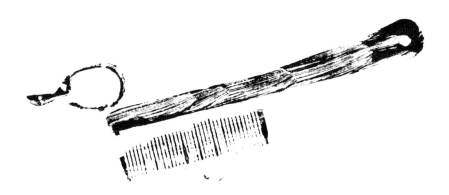

DRAWING

Materials needed.
Hard and soft lead pencils; ball point and nib and holder pens; markers with different sized tips; round and flat brushes; drawing or writing ink; black and white poster paint; all kinds of paper and board, some smooth and some with a rough tooth, or surface.

Drawing is the use of line to create a design or picture. There are many types of drawing. Some are like thinking with a pencil; they are notes or visual ideas. Others are complete in themselves. They are not a study or preparation for something, but are total expressions in themselves. All artists have used drawing to make idea-notes. Some artists are famous for their work in line as a total art form.

When books were still being hand lettered they were often decorated with lovely line drawings. Beautiful examples from the past have been left by artists such as Michelangelo and Rembrandt. Modern artists are still experimenting with new drawing techniques.

Scribbling is a good drawing exercise that will loosen up the hand and the mind at the same time. Cover several pages with scribbles. Use them to get ideas. Find faces or add them until a whole crowd seems to fill the page.

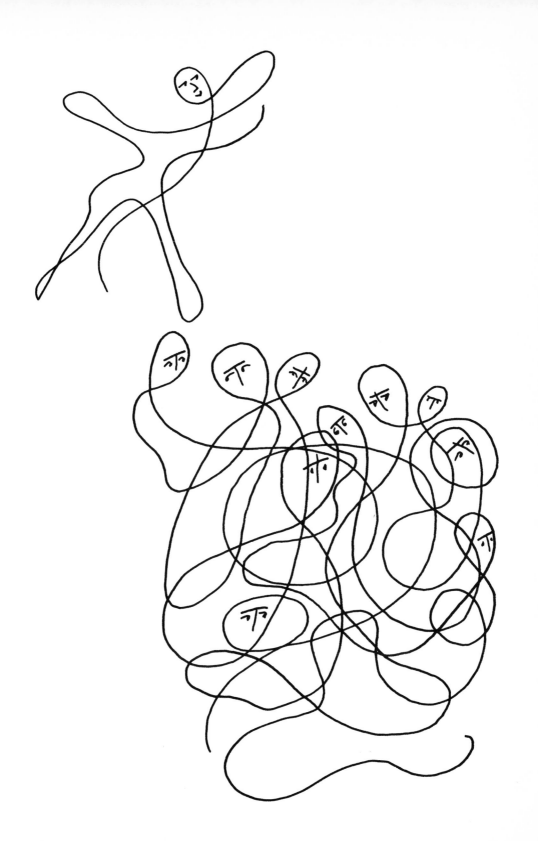

Another drawing exercise is to use a series of lines to indicate a figure. This is called action drawing because it is done very fast, and because the figures look as if they were in motion. Action drawing is almost like making figures of bundles of straw. With practice you will get very good at putting your ideas on paper before they fly out of your head. And by writing them down in this way, you can keep a kind of picture diary of your thoughts.

When you are drawing, you need to create a sense of depth in order to have a place to put things on your paper. The simplest way to do this is to make a division between the sky and the ground. This is called the horizon line. If it is placed high on the page there will be more ground, and you will have more room to stand things. If it is lower there will be more empty space or sky. Anything above the horizon line that is not connected to the ground will float, like a balloon or clouds. Make a series of different horizons and feel the way the ground and sky seem to change.

Once you see the way the horizon functions, add simple forms like rectangles. The more variety of size and shape there is the better. Place them in back of one another. Let the front rectangles block out those behind them. Pile them up. See how many you can get on a page, and notice the feeling of depth. Some seem to go back *into* the paper, while others seem to press forward.

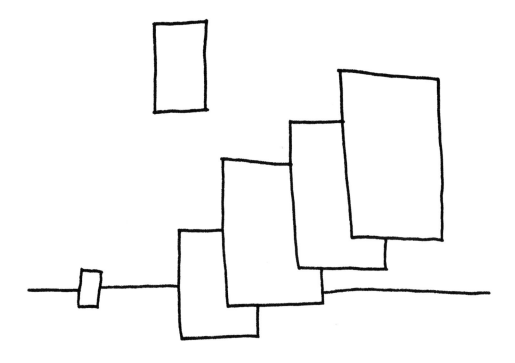

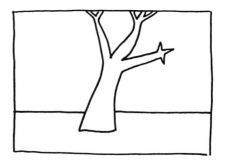

By this time, you may have noticed that groups of things are more interesting than one thing by itself. A drawing of a tree may be very nice, but there will probably be too much empty paper, with nothing happening. If you make trees, make ten or twelve until you have no more room. Or draw a close knit group of shapes and then turn them into things afterward. They can become almost anything, from plants to people. Try a group of forms and see what they suggest.

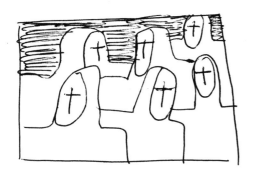

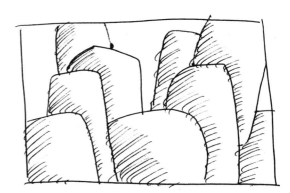

In order to really use people in a picture, try this idea. First, think of each figure as standing, sitting, or lying down. Then, make a shape that fits each of these positions, that is, straight up and down, bent, or flattened out on the ground. Place three or four of these shapes on a page and add a horizon line behind them. Now add faces, arms and legs, and clothing. Keep the whole thing very simple. And try to keep your additions inside each shape rather than sticking limbs on. This will make them stronger and better designed. Make a group of wild shapes and then "see" the figures hidden within them.

49

Sometimes a combination of landscape and still life works better than either one by itself. If objects are placed on a table or shelf in front of a window, the things that are close, and therefore larger looking, contrast with those that are far away, like mountains, trees, or clouds. Notice the difference between the light pen lines and the heavier brush marks. Each has its own quality and feeling. Use the one that works best in your picture.

Outside and inside, far and near, are contrasting forms. As you have seen, contrasts increase the dramatic impact of a picture. In this experiment a strong, blocklike image of buildings is partially blocked by curved, natural forms. When the mechanical building shapes are slightly hidden by the free linear movements of the trees, the one increases the qualities of the other. Try other combinations that are opposite to one another and see what happens.

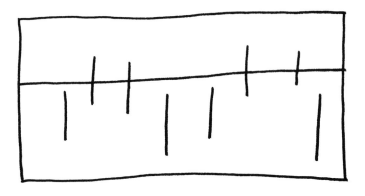

When you are drawing, you will discover that a slanted line creates a tipped plane and increases the feeling of depth. It is a kind of perspective. The higher up on the paper that lines are placed, the further away they seem to be. Make a series of straight lines going up and down across the page. Then connect the top and bottom of each line to the one next to it. Keep the lines parallel. You will have made a kind of zig zag wall or fence. Put a painting on each section and you will have your own outdoor art show.

Now make a double line to resemble a rope or vine. Visualize a thick line going over and under itself. Interweave many of these ropelike movements and turn the whole thing into a jungle scene.

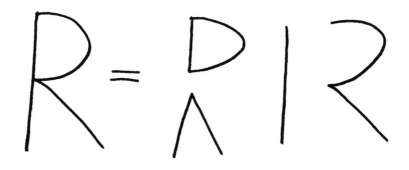

Letters are very clear, simple designs. In order to see how good they are, try taking some apart. This is similar to finding themes in music that are repeated in variations throughout the work. Good strong designs can be made in this way, and sometimes turned into fascinating pictures.

59

To make an ordinary drawing of simple objects exciting, try this. First make a group of things like tools, fruit, kitchen utensils, plants, or even people. Make a very thick black outline around each one. Next, take a brush and white paint and fill in each thing until hardly any of the outline is left. The finished result will be that of the white swelling over on top of the black lines rather than the usual lines resting on the paper. This will make each object appear to have more depth or dimension.

Most drawings are made of black lines on white paper. But let's try something different. Draw a picture on a black or dark-colored paper. Use a pen and white ink or a pointed brush with white or light-colored paint. Each line seems to "jump" out against the background. By changing an ordinary approach to drawing you can grasp the way techniques are related to seeing habits. A simple reversing of light and dark can bring about an unexpected reaction and a new kind of surprise.

Now try this combination. Paste a large, irregular, dark shape on white paper. This will make a strong abstract design. Then draw a scene by using a dark line on the white areas and a light line on the dark areas. As the line shifts from light to dark, the image will change in a new and powerful way. Continue experimenting with various kinds of lines, dark and light shapes, textures, and images. Look at drawings by artists of all periods and see if you can find ideas and techniques for your own use.

THRee-DiMENSioNAL FoRMS

Materials needed.
Bits of wood and small wooden objects, like spools and blocks; wire or wire coat hangers; cardboard of all thicknesses; boxes of different sizes; newspapers; plaster; wheat paste and a strong glue; wire cutters; pliers; a stapler; tape; sand or gravel such as used in bird cages; paint and brushes.

Three-dimensional art is closer to sculpture than painting or drawing. It can be done on a flat base, but the design is raised and is touchable.

In ancient times, figures and decorations were cut into walls to form relief patterns. Then sculptured figures of men and women were made part of the buildings, and used as columns or to hold up the roof. Eventually some stone or bronze images of people and animals were made to stand by themselves. Later, statues were sprinkled through gardens, parks, and cities for everyone to enjoy.

In creating three-dimensional forms, the feeling-difference is mostly that of being able to handle or touch each surface. You must learn a new way to think about each work. Actual materials are used instead of paintings of these materials. Real wood is used rather than an imitation of wood grain. There is also a real light and shade that make the shapes stand out in relief.

In order to see how forms catch light and throw shadows try this simple relief made of cardboard. Once again contrasts are needed. Cut out a series of six or more irregular, mountainlike forms. Glue these one by one between flat blocks of wood that are cut the same length as the cardboard pieces. Since the irregular forms are upright, they become verticals. The alternating flat wood strips turn into a horizontal base. Paint each strip a different color, or paint the whole thing white and watch the shadows change as it is moved under different lights.

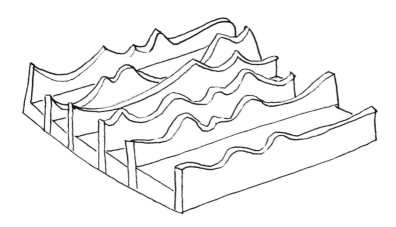

To make a more specific image, like a face, cut a series of cardboard rectangles, squares, or windowlike shapes. Decide how they are to go, color them, and glue them into place. For extra thickness sandwich a couple of layers of board together. Once again place the light above, then below, or to the right, then to the left. Watch how the cast shadows change and become an important part of your composition.

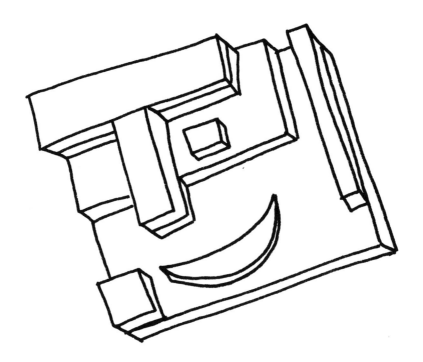

Now we will try a textural surface: a sand painting. The effect of light on this rough physical material is very different than on smooth surfaces. The American Indians used colored sand to make ritual designs.

On a heavy piece of cardboard or plywood, paint a thick coat of glue. While the glue is wet, sprinkle the surface with sand. Bird gravel works very well. When dry, turn it over and hit the back until all the excess sand falls off. Then paint a design in color on this sandy background. Place the finished work in a good light so that the texture shows to the best advantage.

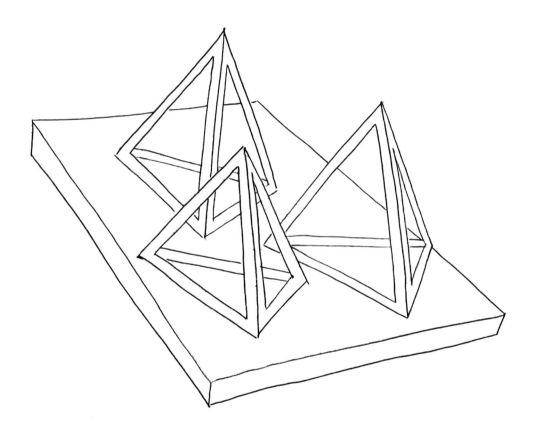

Sometimes it is easier to show the three-dimensional qualities of an object if it is less than solid. By this I mean that an object with a hollow core, or with holes in it, has more of a feeling of taking up space. The empty surrounding atmosphere seems to flow through the form, and it is easier to see how it fills more room. Try and get the feel of several of these hollow shapes so they can be seen through one another in a compositional manner. Use several forms of the same type, or different from one another. Color them and glue them to a base.

These can also be suspended by wire or cord to float in ever-changing combinations.

  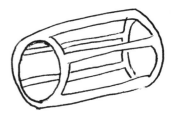

In this experiment, objects are used that suggest an image. Plastic or wooden spoons look a little like people. If you paint or use markers to make faces on them, they can easily turn into a crowd. Take the lid of a box and fill it with plaster. While it is wet stick these people-spoons into it. The more spoons the better. When the plaster is dry, paint it to look like water and you will have a happy group of bathers. See how many things around the house can be turned into scenes like this.

Cardboard or paper can also be bent into three-dimensional shapes. All kinds of interesting images can be made with folded forms. Look at this bull's head and see what you can make up.

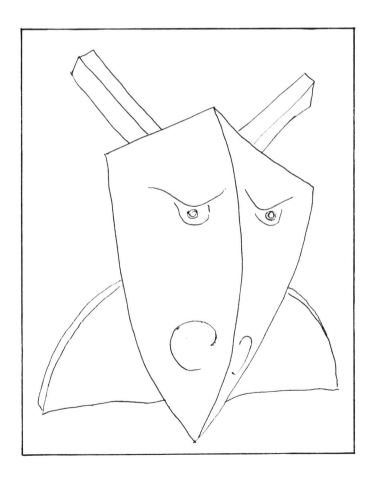

A head is very hard to imagine. But if you think of masks from Africa or the South Sea Islands, or Indian Totems, you will be able to make an image that is rough but very effective.

For a start, take a box and glue a couple of things in it, like spools, for the eyes. Then find something for the nose and mouth. Children's blocks work very well. Make a collection of things that will give you ideas for these object-images.

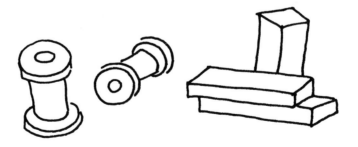

This head is made of bent wire. It is a sort of bird-cage head. Since this is a see-through idea, you can even hang some inner thoughts inside. Use wire that is easy to bend with simple pliers. A little glue will hold it in place at each crossing, or they can be tied with thread. How many creatures can you make in this manner? Remember it is a little like drawing in space. It is a three-dimensional line.

Papier mâché is a French term for a mixture of glue and paper that can be molded into a strong, light, three-dimensional form. It is especially good for making masks.

Bend and tape strips of light cardboard into place to form a base for your mask. If it is to be worn, wrap the strip of board around your face so that it will fit. Next make a mixture of flour and water, or wallpaper paste. Then tear news paper into long strips, dip them into the paste and lay them *across* the cardboard base. Pile layer after layer across one another, brushing extra paste on if needed. The features can be smoothed, roughened, or built up as needed. Holes should be left for the eyes or they can be made to pop out or sink in, depending on the expression you have in mind. You can also mount your mask on a base or hang it up as a sculptural object.
Let the whole thing dry until hard. It can then be painted. You can also use a soft clay that does not dry, called plasteline, to mold the face with more detail, or use the clay as a base for the mask. When the paper strips are dry, the modeling clay should be scraped out. Colored paper, or some that is striped or even patterned, can be used so that it is unnecessary to paint.

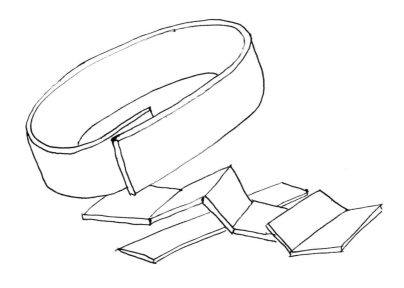

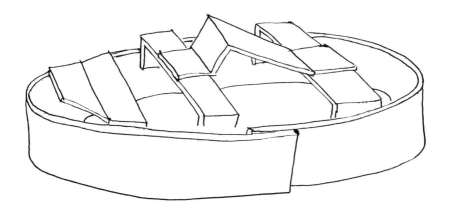

Figures are the most difficult of all things to do. Yet empty boxes can be glued together to form a great figure—a statue of boxes. Study the example and create your own figures in all kinds of positions. Give it a wild costume—even a tattoo—with paint.

If you need a special size box, make one. Cut the shapes as shown and tape them together. Use the central rectangle to measure the size you need.

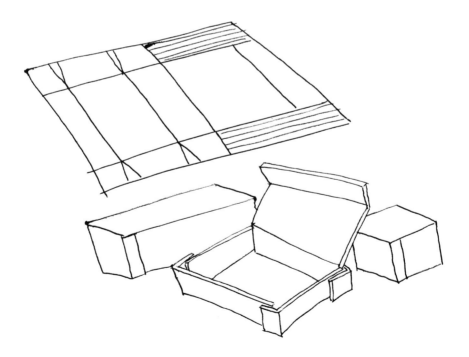

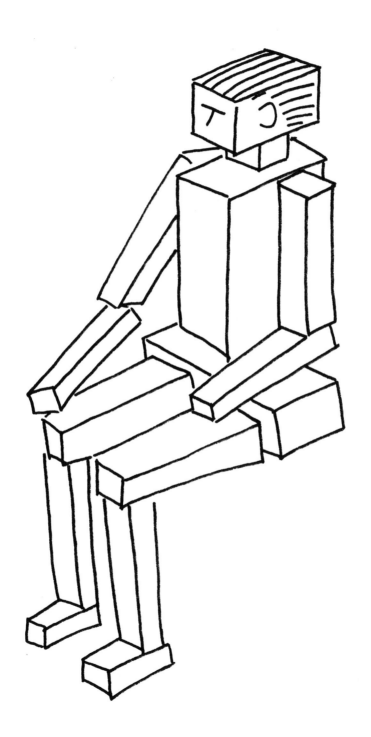

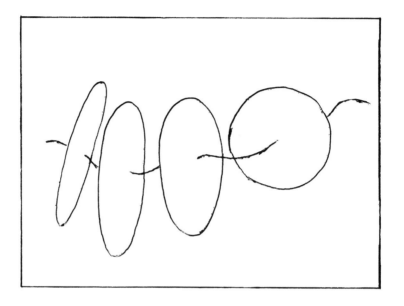

Using cardboard disks, you can make a puppetlike figure. Cut the disks with scissors. Change the sizes so that they make up the different parts of the body. Then string them together with a strong needle and thread. The result will be an image that is not stationary. It can be hung up and moved. It therefore comes under the heading of movable sculpture.

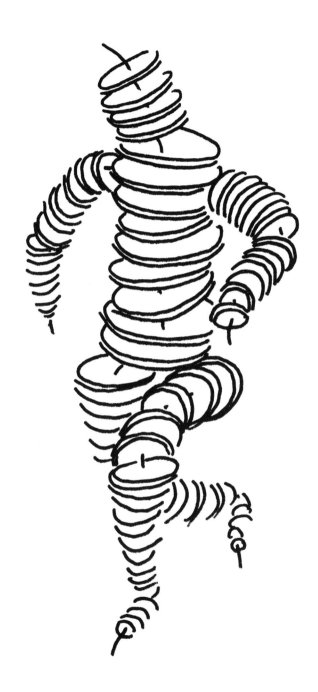

Many simple, ordinary forms can be used as a basic shape and support for sculpture. Once the support is fastened to a base, a variety of materials can be used to build up an image. Plaster, papier mâché, plastic wood, self-hardening clay, even plaster impregnated bandage that is used by doctors for making casts on broken bones can be used. Let the simple form act as a skeletonlike core. Turn a piece of wire or metal into a deer. A bent piece of angle iron, like that used to hold up a shelf, can become a seated figure. See what ideas you can get from odds and ends around the house or garage.

Here an old glass, bottle, or tin can is turned into a sculptured animal vase. Using the clean jar, or what-have-you, as a base, pack plaster or papier mâché around it until it turns into a strange bird or animal. Paint it in colors that are unreal in order to underline its fantasy quality.

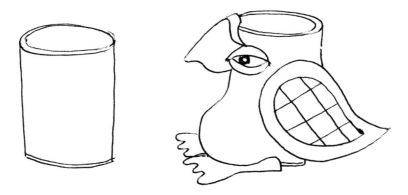

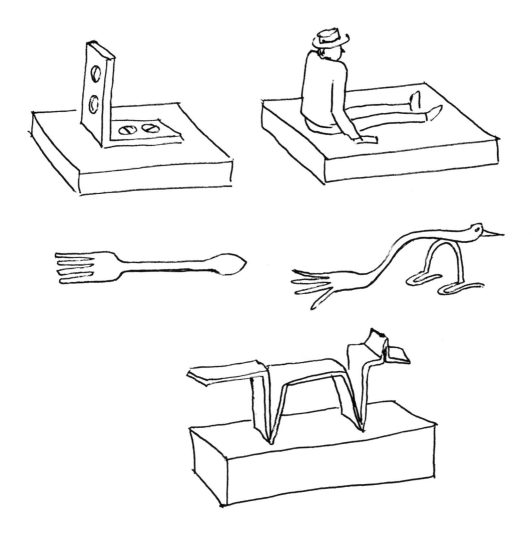

Three-dimensional materials that can be swung around, or hung up and blown by the wind, are moving sculptures. They are called mobiles.

Try combinations of these arrangements. Use wire and strong, colored cardboard. Light plastic that can be cut with a scissors is also good to use. The ends of each arm or branch can be formed into a loop and hooked into the next branch. If you start at the lower form and work toward the top, it will be easier to balance the whole work. The stand can be made of a firm piece of wood fastened securely to a base. Two interlocked triangles of cardboard can also be glued to a base and painted.

In order to hang mobiles try this idea. Push the wire arms through a corrugated board cut as shown. This can then be moved up or down to insure the balance that is needed. Try strange shapes that vary at the ends of each wire. Make them really different in size, some large, some tiny. If one side of a fin is painted white and the other black, or in contrasting stripes or patterns, they will make a dramatic change as they turn and flip by.

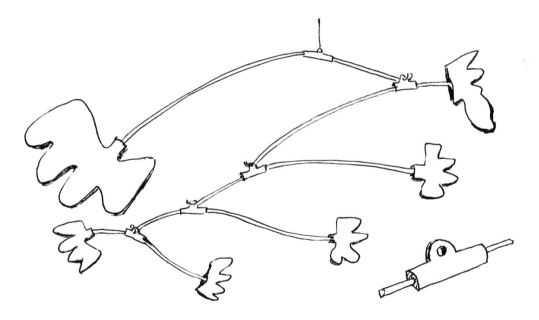

Although these projects have been separated into four general groups, they are meant to work with one another. An idea for a three-dimensional form may trigger an idea for a print. An idea for a print may be the start of a series of drawings. When it comes to exercising your creativity there are no boundaries. The whole world is open to you. Use the things around you and the things within you to express yourself in as many languages as possible. You are the real product of art.